MOUTH:
EATS
COLOR

MOUTH: EATS COLOR

SAGAWA CHIKA TRANSLATIONS, ANTI-TRANSLATIONS & ORIGINALS BY

SAWAKO NAKAYASU
W/ CHIKA SAGAWA

ROGUE FACTORIAL
2011

FOR THE ROGUE QUEEN VIOLET JUNO

PROMENADE

季節は　　　　　手袋はめかへ
Seasons change their gloves
　　　　　　　　　　in

　　報道を埋める花びらの　　fading

afternoon　　　　　薄れ日の

　　午後三時　　　　　　light

　　白と黒とのスクリイン

瞳は雲に蔽はれて　the day clouds over

　　　　　　約束も
with nothing left to vow　　ない日がくれる

黒い空気

夕暮が遠くで太陽の舌を切る。

水の中では空の街々が笑ふことをやめる。

総ての影が樹の上から降りて来て私をとりまく。林や窓硝子は
女のやうに青ざめる。夜は完全にひろがつた。乗合自動車は
焔をのせて公園を横切る。

その時私の感情は街中を踊りまはる

悲しみを追ひ出すまで。

プロムナアド

セイゾン は　グローブはめかへ

　　　　レポートを 埋める　フラワーの

フェーディング

午後　　　　　　スリーオクロック
　　　　　ブランとノワールの
　　　　　　　　　　　スクリイン

アイ　　は

ヌアージュに蔽はれて

プロメッスもない　　　　ジュールがくれる

GLASS WING

This is what the sun destroys on the street corner, easily: love, smashed between glass wings, previously passed along among the people—gently, gently.

This is what the sky faces: the window, darkening with each rotation of the ventilator.

This is what the rooftop leans on: a single line drawn between one leaf in the sky and another.

This is what the trains creep alongside of: swelling streets.

This is where the sailor's collar spins: between the blue wrinkles in the sky. Between the blue wrinkles in the sky. Collar of the sailors laughing in the place of a yawn.

Everybody now: wear your summer finest and get in line. Here is your flask, now get inside. Will you crumble. Perhaps. Is this what you would call a happy shadow. A shadow of happiness. Does it rain. Does it fruit. Is this my heart and why do I feel so—

PROMENADE

The saisons changent their 手袋
A trois o'clock
薄れ日の
Petals des fleurs that bury leur report
ホワイト and ブラックの screen
Les yeux covered par the nuages
Evening se couche on some jours sans プロミス.

IF WE EMPTY OUT ALL THIS AIR WILL IT FINALLY GO BLACK

There are cities whose laughter is cut short by the encroaching water.

I unleash my emotions
Which run rampant through the streets
Noising away all grief and sorrow.

Trees, hold on to your shadows.
Windows, go pale.
Forests, go long—like women.

The moment when nightspread completes itself.

Passenger: you.
Passenger: myself.
Passenger: non-solitary flame.
All go galloping across the park.

(Allow me to cut your tongue off, little sparrow.)

Remove the speech of the sun, but please do it at a distance, old dusk.

ガラスの翼

人々が大切さうに渡していつた硝子の翼にはさんだ恋を、
太陽は街かどで毀してしまふ。

空は窓に向つて立つてゐる、ヴエンチレエタアのまはるたびに
いろが濃くなる。

木の葉は空にある、それは一本の棒を引いてゐる、屋根らは
凭りかかつて。

ふくらんだ街路を電車は匍ひ、空中の青い皺の間を旋廻
する水兵の襟。

盛装して夏の行列は通りすぎフラスコの中へ崩れる。

私らの心の果実は幸福な影を降らしてゐる。

PROMENADE (PUROMUNAADO 1)

Season bag
Reported buried in flower
Thin day
Three o'clock afternoon
Black screen white
Hitomi cloud cover
Sunset bound

BEARD OF DEATH

A chef clutches the blue sky. Four fingerprints are left,

——Gradually a chicken sheds blood. Even here the sun is crushed.

Blue-suited wardens of the sky who inquire.

I hear daylight run by.

In prison they keep watch over a dream longer than life.

A moth slams into the window so as to touch the outside world, like the backside of an embroidery.

If for a single day the long whisker of death would loosen its hold, this miracle would make us jump with joy.

Death strips my shell.

プロムナアド (PUROMUNAADO 2)

季節手袋
報道埋花
薄日
午後三時
白黒幕
瞳雲覆
約束日暮

BLACK AIR

In the distance, dusk cuts the tongue of the sun.

Underwater, town after town in the sky stops laughing.

All shadows drop from the trees and gang up on me. Forests and windowpanes go pale, like a woman. Night has spread completely. The carpool takes a flame aboard and crosses the park.

At that point my emotions dance about the city

Until they have driven out the grief.

PROMENADE (PUROMUNAADO 3)

Seasonal gloves
Flowers embedding media
Trace of sun
At 3:00 pm
White mastermind
Clouds covered the pupil
Higurashi promise

GLASS WING

People carefully pass along love, held between glass wings, which the sun destroys on the street corner.

The sky stands facing the window, darkening as the ventilator turns.

Leaves are in the sky, drawing a single line, the rooftops leaning in.

Trains crawl along the bulging street, the sailor's collar rotating between blue creases in the sky.

The dressed up lines of summer pass by and crumble into the flask.

The fruits of our hearts rain happy shadows.

プロムナアド (PUROMUNAADO 4)

季　節 手
袋報 道埋
花 薄 日
午 後 三 時
白 黒 幕
瞳 雲
覆約 束日 暮

死の髯

料理人が青空を握る。四本の指跡がついて、

——次第に鶏が血をながす。ここでも太陽はつぶれてゐる。

たづねてくる青服の空の看守。

日光が駆け脚でゆくのを聞く。

彼らは生命よりながい夢を牢獄の中で守つてゐる。

刺繍の裏のやうな外の世界に触れるために一匹の蛾となつて
窓に突きあたる。

死の長い巻鬚が一日だけしめつけるのをやめるならば私らは
奇蹟の上で跳びあがる。

死は私の殻を脱ぐ。

PROMENADE (PUROMENAADO 5)

Seasonal hand
Road information buried bags
Sun flower light
After three-time meridian
Black Curtain
Eye Cloud
Sun late capping promise

DARK SONG

Upon the new carpet all abloom
Quietly slowly
Two donkeys push a lorry.
On the street where the proud flower petals burn
Silk feathers are dyed by pollen.
And where her toes touch
A white rainbow is portrayed.

PROMENADE (PUROMUNAADO 6)

Wear gloves to do the seasonal
The petals fill the news
Faded day
At 3:00 pm
Screen of white and black
Swollen eyes are on cloud cover
Promise me no day

A BEARD OF DEATH GROWS ON ME

To make food while gripping the astounding blue sky.

Consider all that is killed, including the less astounding sun.

Consider all who are charged with protecting or sheltering

In the face of escaping daylight.

This dream lasts longer than your sentence

As was confirmed by a moth at the extremities of this embroidered world.

My beard tightens its grip on me.

Would I escape it if I could.

As death, I shake off this shell.

PROMENADE (PUROMUNAADO 7)

Portez des gants pour ne saisonnières
Les pétales de remplir les nouvelles
Jour fané
À 15:00
Ecran de blanc et noir
Yeux gonflés sont sur le nuage 蔽
Promets-moi pas un jour

暗い歌

咲き揃つた新しいカアペツトの上を
二匹の驢馬がトロツコを押して行く
静かに　ゆつくりと
奢れる花びらが燃えてゐる道で
シルクの羽は花粉に染まり
彼女の爪先がふれる處は
白い虹がゑがかれる。

プロムナアド (PUROMUNAADO 8)

季節を避けるために手袋を着用してください
新しいを埋めるために花びら
デイは色あせた
15:00
画面の黒と白
腫れた目は、クラウド上にある蔽
私は一日ではない約束

昆虫

昆虫が電流のやうな速度で繁殖した。
地殻の腫物をなめつくした。

美麗な衣装を裏返して、都会の夜は女のやうに眠つた。

私はいま殻を乾す。
鱗のやうな皮膚は金属のやうに冷たいのである。

顔半面を塗りつぶしたこの秘密をたれもしつてはゐないのだ。

夜は、盗まれた表情を自由に廻転さす痣のある女を有頂天に
する。

PROMENADE (PUROMUNAADO 9)

Please wear gloves in order to evade the seasons
Flower petals to bury the new
Day has faded
Three o'clock
Black and white of the screen
Swollen eyes are a shield abouve the clouds
I am a promise that goes beyond a single day

WATCH

Having one day heard the tale of Tehching Hsieh and his Cage piece, the ant was relieved to learn of a friend, at least one other being out there, who might possibly know how this feels. The second hand is relentless, after all. The ant has a total of two options, three if you count the option created by the combination of the first two.

Option #1 is colloquially referred to as the jumprope method, which is valued for the 59 seconds of rest and relaxation offered within the bounds of every single minute. On the other hand, like a Little League right fielder, the long bouts between action carries with it the danger of a wandering imagination, lack of attention, straying vision, all of which could lead to serious injury and loss, should the second hand arrive at an inopportune moment.

(continued on page 33)

Cloud-form / Delicate fingertip, like a leaf.

Rush through the 鈴 まの arches so that the
sparse rows i teeming rows of silver people might
くぐる pass through, to 行き, を excavate.

Memory breaks down into くだけたた rocks and trees, and stars,
くだ (a tube), けた (a decade or order of magnitude),
above the stars and all, a dried up brilliance,
星 以上に かがやく 物 qui brille.

To wit, 書いて:
To wit, カマテニ is 悠 @ gathered のとば near で
   and then torn away
   そして かぎ さかれる。
   and then ga gathered away.

(VERSUS)

City of marble, a great logical stone, 大理石 の建ち姿
作る a made constructed light emission
   a circulation l flower,
      wreath, はげ付
      + style つくつの sway.

毎 (My) Every day a 日 (nichi),
      the map (chisel) drawn by a
         はのようでて こまかい のびてる。

WATCH (CONTINUED)

Option #2, the walk-behind method (with a shout-out to Yoko Ono's "Bottoms" movie), is quite to the contrary, and involves a continuous forward motion reminiscent of that undertaken by domesticated hamsters. By means of a circular walking path at a radius of 1cm from the center and covering six degrees of the circle per second, the ant is able to follow the second hand consistently, without fail. It is even reminded of bygone days foraging with the colony, marching along at a regular pace.

(continued on page 36)

DARK SONG

Two donkeys push, yes push, heave, a lorry, yes quietly, gently, above the newness of the carpet that has filled and bloomed, filled and bloomed, with plumb and abandon, where the pride of the flower petals burns up the street, where the pollen stains all the feathers, and where her toes touch, a white rainbow, touch a white rainbow, now draw it.

O, decrepit vast haze of winter ——
毎年土をかぶらせてね

The hair on your head has driedものうげに跫音もたてず

Crouched beside the road いけがきの忍冬にすがりつき
Listlessly walking silently, 道ばたにうづくまつてしまふ
Clinging to the honeysuckle on the hedge ——
おいぼれの冬よ
PLEASE COVER WITH DIRT EVERY YEAR
—— おまへの頭髪はかわいて

And the people who walked above it
その上をあるいた人も
Have died, along with their memories.
それらの思ひ出も死んでしまつた。

WATCH (CONTINUED)

The combination method was developed as the legs on the ant started to falter, as the legs on the left side grew about 30% more muscular than those on the right while at the same time on the brink of exhaustion-collapse, even after the development of a system of walking backwards in order to relieve the accrual of muscular imbalance between the right and left sides of the body. Such a method combines all the long-term benefits of the walk-behind method, which allows for the longest period of time with no direct needle contact, with the true repose offered by the jumprope method. The successful implementation of this method involves achieving enough tiredness during the duration of the walk-behind method, so as to fall asleep right into the jumprope method, having entered a sleep so deep that one is able to jump over the approaching second hand while hardly disturbing its sleep, in fact continuing right on with the sleep, as can be attested to by the continuity of the dream therein experienced. This combination method has its dangers, however, and one is advised never to try this first, but only after much experience and familiarity with the jumprope method has been achieved.

(continued on page 39)

CLOUD-FORM/ DELICATE FINGERTIP, LIKE A LEAF

Push through the 銀色の arches so that the rows upon teeming rows of silver people might とほる pass through, to ほる, excavate.

Memory breaks down into くだけた rocks and trees and stars, くだ (a tube), けた (a decade or order of magnitude), above the stars and all, a dried-up brilliance, 星以上に輝くモノ qui brille.

To wit, wrinkle: カアテン (rideaux), ルドンの窓,
gathered near のそばで

and then torn away そして引き裂かれる and then
gathered away.

City of marble, a great logical stone,
versus
大理石の街が作る
constructed new emission of light
circulation of flower

                                        a single sway

毎日 my—itchy—every day—the map (chizu)—drawn by a—葉のような、細かい指先.

WIDOW'S JAZZ   BY MINA LOY

White flesh, black soul, trembles—Chicago! Chicago!—
this yowl I do not know—shift tangle pale snakes —
return to a primitive border, ecstatic stupor—white
cleverness puts an end to this movement by colored
people holding moonlight in their eyes—possessed
by an elegant harmonium in the woods—wooden
flute of maiden sapling—gigolos massage, wander
diagonal—towards crying taboo—electric crown—pul-
verizes the products of the floor's secrets—a pruned
shape melts into dissonant pearl—plate—trans-
gresses—a mature eros—spinning a comedic actor—
black animal angels—find human gloves—barking
inside the strange largeness of a metal torso—and
then—prankster music—facing a flock of fainted
pigeons—entranced leisure is smashed to pieces—
unfair—enormous—absentee—darkness of the substi-
tute—tumble into incandescent-like memory—survi-
vors of love—regarding this rich martyrdom—burned
by the flames of music—the widowed coffin—your slain
laughter supports it powerlessly—O good person—
how secretly you betrayed me with death—when
this some jazz—blows upon this tropical heat—
between the resonance of flesh—racial caress—synthe-
size—angels and donkeys—unmistakable esperanto
of this earth—converse—unending joy—when my
desires—reach—the distance of death—I search—half-
opaque silence —for a space without human shadow

WATCH (CONTINUED)

In fact it is the invention of this, the combination method, which allows the ant to live well over the 20-day estimate (according to myrmecologists) until one day I wake up and get ready for work as usual, and when I put on my watch, I see that the ant has developed a new system altogether, and we exchange a few quick words as I walk out the door.

PROMENADE (A)

Seasons change their gloves
A three o'clock
Trace of sun
Of flower petals which bury their report
A black and white screen
Eyes covered by clouds
Some promise-less day comes to an end

毎年土をかぶらせてね

ものうげに跫音もたてず
いけがきの忍冬にすがりつき
道ばたにうづくまつてしまふ
おいぼれの冬よ
おまへの頭髪はかわいて
その上をあるいた人も
それらの思ひ出も死んでしまつた。

PROMENADE (B)

Seasons replace their gloves
The fading light
At three o'clock
On flowers filling the news
A black and white screen
Eyes are covered by clouds at
The end of a day without promise

雲のかたち

銀色の波のアアチをおしあけ
行列の人々がとほる。

くだけた記憶が石と木と星の上に
かがやいてゐる。

皺だらけのカアテンが窓のそばで
集められそして引き裂かれる。

大理石の街がつくる放射光線の中を
ゆれてゆく一つの花環

毎日、葉のやうな細い指先が
地図をかいてゐる。

PROMENADE (C)

Seasons remplace   gloves

      fading light

three o'clock

      flowers fill the nouvelles

a black and white screen

      eyes
          covered by clouds   at

   the end of a day   sans

         promise

INSECTS

Speed of electrical currents generated by insects as
they proliferate on my skin
    analogous to:

Speed of insects devouring this ground-tumor
    in contrast to:

Speed of my shell drying outside
    and:

Speed of heat transfer between my metal skin and
your scaly skin

To reverse this gorgeous dress of yours
Into a city, a sleeping woman, night—

I do not know if this secret covers half my face
Or if half my face is surface enough to contain this
matter of confidence.

What makes the bruised woman ecstatic.
Steal her expression and fling it about—
O Night—

SHAPE OF CLOUDS

The silver arched wave is pushed open,
Rows of people walk through.

Broken-down memory sparkles
above the rocks, the trees, the stars.

A wrinkled curtain near the window
Is gathered, then pulled apart.

A single garland sways in the radiant rays of light
made by the city of marble.

Every day, fingertips thin like a leaf
Are drawing a map.

PROMENADE (Pろめなで)

背亜損sちゃん下テェイrgろゔぇs

アthレエお′cろck

Tら背尾fすn

オffロウェrペタlsウィch部ryテェイれぽrt

アbらck案dウィテscれえn

エィェsコヴェレdbycろうds

染めp路店—レッs打y混めsとあんえんd

WHITE FIRE   BY HARRY CROSBY

In my dreams your throat is a fleeting brilliance of emotion. Which is why I am always shot past the point of awakening, ruled by the moving pictures of this white fire.

PROMENADE (露命撫で)

背亜損(せあそん) 銭(ちゃん) 下(した) 手酔ひ(てえい)炉辺
(ろべ) 吾(あ) 令(れい) 悪露(おろ)

羅(ら) 脊尾(せお) 押(おす)

小呂(おろ) 上(うえ) ペタ(ぺた) 浮い(うい) 部(ぶ) 手酔ひ(て
えい) レポ(れぽ)

あら 浮いて(ういて) 列絵(れえ)

永(えい) 子べ(こべ) 老(ろう)

染め(そめ) 露天(ろてん) 列(れつ)打(うつ) 混め(こめ) と(と)、
案縁(あんえん)

GATE OF SNOW

その家のまはりには人の吉びた恩惟がつみあげられてゐる。
Rather pale like a gravestone.
夏は涼しく、冬には温い。
For a moment, I thought—花が咲いたと思つた。
It was a flock of aging snow.

PROMENADE (PASS THE HAND OVER A LIFE AS FLEETING AS THE DEW)

A back turned on subsequent loss of money
under the drunken hand of rovers
in the vicinity of fire.
Order the lochia, such evil dew, out.
The lightest of fabrics push at my backside, tail.
A small low note clinging up above, oui, in this room,
drunk in the hand of the report.

O—float—row of paintings
Eternal aging child
Steeped, exposed to the sky
a row of hits crowd around
the idea of a fortunate tie.

午後

花びらの如く降る。
重い重量にうたれて昆虫は木陰をおりる。
牆壁に集まるもの、微風のうしろ、日射が波が響をころす。
骨骼が白い花をのせる。
思念に遮られて魚が断崖をのぼる。

INSECTS

Insects multiplied with the speed of an electric current.

Lapped up the boils on the earth's crust.

Turning over its exquisite costume, the urban night slept like a woman.

Now I hang my shell out to dry.

My scaly skin is cold like metal.

No one knows this secret half-covering my face.

The night makes the bruised woman, freely twirling her stolen expression, ecstatic.

ANIMAL MAGNETISM   BY HARRY CROSBY

All the sailors laugh. The laughter is contagious. All the prostitutes have fainted. The fainting is contagious. We grow tired from trying to continue laughing and fainting all through the night.

PROMENADE

Construe the report buried by flower petals as one of pressing news—but the gunfire at the back of my throat claims an otherward disclosure. So much for the delicate flowers. The ant in the piece called "Watch" now emerges to point out that three o'clock in the afternoon only takes place for the duration of one second out of 86,400 in a day. Now conjure Chris Burden—not of the shooting piece, but of the five-second black and white television advertising slot he purchased. Five times as long in duration as the reported three o'clock in the afternoon, and someone gets on the telephone with a complaint: why take things so literally?

Cloud cover—are they the same evil clouds who hover over ants taking swim lessons in the wet puddle of an oil painting, or is cover more feasible in the form of a blanket of woven ants—because the day makes no promises, regardless of season.

PLEASE COVER WITH DIRT EVERY YEAR

Listlessly walking silently,
Clinging to the honeysuckle on the hedge
Crouched beside the road
O, decrepit old winter—
The hair on your head has dried
And the people who walked above it
Have died, along with their memories.

プロムナアド

季節は手袋はめかへ
報道を埋める花びらの
薄れ日の
午後三時
白と黒とのスクリイン
瞳は雲に蔽はれて
約束もない日がくれる

SWIMMING IN THE PRESENCE OF LURID OPPOSITION

Summer camp, swim class, Tokyo, a group of no more than twenty ants all donning their respective swimming caps, some with images of their favorite anime characters printed on the fabric. Forward progression, assisted by a rhythmic movement of ant limbs, just like the instructor instructed, forward forward progress, forward forward progress. The slowness, agonizing slowness of such, such poor swimmers these ants, most likely in the beginner class for sad ants with little ability. And then the However, the Big But, the Truth that reveals itself

(continued on page 66)

5 8

雪の門

その家のまはりには人の古びた思惟がつみあげられてゐる。
——もはや墓石のやうにあをざめて。
夏は涼しく、冬には温い。
私は一時、花が咲いたと思つた。
それは年とつた雪の一群であつた。

UNTITLED POEM   BY FRANCES CHUNG

My Italian girlfriends dressed up on Sundays in dresses and heels. They told me they were going to eat chinks after confession. I thought that this was either someone's house or the name of a restaurant. Little did I know they were headed for Chinatown. Not having any spending money, and never going to church, I never joined them. We went our separate ways on Sundays.

WAVES

The sailors are laughing.
With their teeth bared,
Like on the barrel organs
Thrashing about all over the place.
Unflaggingly
They press the bellows with their entire bodies
While laughter passes from shore to shore.

The laughter we have today
Is captive to the eternal
And silence only grows deeper still.
Because the tongue is simple, like a pair of clappers.
Now, people
Simply open their mouths
As when yawning.

GATE OF SNOW

People's outdated beliefs are piled up around that house.

—— Rather pale like a gravestone.

Cool in summer, warm in winter.

For a moment, I thought flowers had bloomed.

It was a flock of aging snow.

WE THE HEATHENS

Last night we go to have Chinese for dinner and my friend who is visiting from another planet is horrified (and perhaps a little excited also), until I explain to her that we are having Chinese food, not Chinese people. We go to a place that serves not dumpling soup, which I love, but soup dumpling, with which I am unfamiliar. The soup is actually inside of each dumpling, and everyone develops their own system of eating. As we poke our chopsticks voraciously into the folds of the Crispy Fried Whole Exploded Fish, which is delicious, it becomes clear to me that we would have no right to be shocked or mortified or outraged or even surprised or upset, should some creature from another planet descend upon the earth, pluck our people off the ground and fry us up, tearing away at our flesh with relish.

(continued on page 74)

AFTERNOON

Raining like flower petals.
Hit by a heavy weight, insects descend the tree shade.
Gathering at the mast wall, trailing a faint breeze—
Sounds are killed by the sun, the waves.
My skeleton places white flowers upon it.
Interrupted by thoughts, fish climb the cliff.

波

水夫が笑つてゐる。
歯をむきだして
そこらぢゆうのたうちまはつてゐる
バルバリイの風琴のやうに。
倦むこともなく
彼らは全身で蛇腹を押しつつ
笑ひは岸辺から岸辺へとつたはつてゆく。

我々が今日もつてゐる笑ひは
永劫のとりこになり
沈黙は深まるばかりである。
舌は拍子木のやうに単純であるために。
いまでは人々は
あくびをした時のやうに
ただ口をあけてゐる。

SWIMMING IN THE PRESENCE OF LURID OPPOSITION (CONTINUED)

only after zooming out and away from what used to be a close-up shot of ants in an unusually colored swimming pool, such as red or green or pale fuschia or celadon, the distance revealing the inherent difficulty of making a swimming pool out of a still-wet oil painting, the artist and brush hovering nearby like the evil clouds that they are.

FLANKY PONGO (URLA) #8 BY STEVE WILLARD

cantación (liberatura) y un timbó …

                                               Archamosayos .

pidiendo para   vaciar las bandas …

Seguria   la port-únidad itemporal ha
  tomada serial

             (com'un tenue-cellisca
se a'rende en habili,

                marchámor's
      trancelín

  -típlomadas Nastic de San-isla
   contra extractor colgadas ~~enburlándose? moji~~.)

        cretenutas prueban el sol….   retintinín adabanistas tapiocal

o lerda'ica!—debe que, las fósiles y un persón devorar

con basba enclítica; con enclítica, basba….

BACKSIDE

Night eats color
Flower bouquets lose their fake ornaments.
Day falls into the leaves like sparkling fish
The shapeless dreams and trees
Struggle like the lowly mud
Nurtured outside this shriveled, deridable despair.
And the space that was chopped down
Tickles the weeds by its feet.
Fingers stained with cigarette tar
Caress the writhing darkness.
And the people move forward.

FEAR OF COLD

For some reason, I am stranded in an extremely cold environment without my coat, and starting to worry if my life is in danger. After what seems like enough suffering has already taken place, I am fortunate enough to find a house, into which I break in and find a marginal amount of relief. There is nothing at all in the house, there is no power of any kind, and there is a large pile of dead ants near the bathroom door. I am a direct descendant not of MacGyver but his old-fashioned sister, and so I end up using my Other-MacGyver skills to weave a blanket out of the dead ants, which I finish as quickly as I can, and then throw over my body, begging it to bring me warmth. What happens is that I am so grossed out at the fact of having a blanket of ants covering my body, that I quickly grow both sick and intensely anxious about the situation, all of which nervous energy serves to cause the blood cells in my body to vibrate rapidly until I am quite warm, and stay warm until the weather goes warm and I am saved from dying.

THIS AFTERNOON

Rains like flower petals.
Interrupted by whose thoughts—
Fish climb the cliff.

EARLY CONVERSATION   BY MASAKO HIRAIZUMI

A flowing pace that tears easily.

Leaves like sparkling fish.

The sun crawls along the cracked, inflamed hill.

On the burning street, an old woman grows heavy.

The drooping folds of the breeze.

The clouds wilt again, caress the writhing darkness.

Night eats endless color, already lost under the tinny sound of the piano.

A late gathering running across the sky.

Song quiets itself slowly, raining like bones.

In the city the forgotten sounds diminish and distort the distance.

In this way, here, the betrayed and idle beasts tire of sunlight

And hide in the curves of shapeless dreams and trees.

WAVES—A LIST OF CHARACTERS, AND BACKSIDE

Husband of Water: and then the people.

Fresh-Looking Bamboo That Lives Fast and Dies Young: moves forward.

That Which Halts Rice From Growing in the Mouth: caress the writhing darkness.

Harp of Wind: tar from cigarettes.

Person After Handling a Forest Fire: fingers stained.

Skin of Man Who Goes: tickle.

Kingly Human Flesh: these are weeds.

Belly of the Snake: by its feet.

Hand on Armour: and the space beneath

Fresh-Looking Bamboo That Lives Fast and Dies Young: that was chopped down.

Mountain Above the Cliff Under Which We Shield or Hang Out to Dry, Inviolate, While Hurrying the Knife: nurtured outside of.

Myself, Etc: shriveled

The Day That Is Now: deridable despair.

Fresh-Looking Bamboo That Lives Fast and Dies Young: now shapeless

Water That Merges and Flows Vigorously: dreams of trees.

Long Duration of Time It Takes For Energy to Depart: and struggle.

What Sinks Into the Heat of a Black Dog: like the lowly mud.

Water Crowning the Legs of a Tree: day, falls

Tongue: in, into the leaves

White Hand of Wood: like sparkling fish

Single Thread of a Pure Color: flower bouquet

People, Etc: lose their fake ornaments.

Temple of the Day: night.

Mouth: eats color.

WE THE HEATHENS (CONTINUED)

My friend Morton, a sweet and gentle man, is sitting quietly beside me with his uneaten hamburger. I don't know how he managed to get himself a hamburger in a Chinese restaurant, but there he sits, and there sits his hamburger, with the top bun off. Morton says he wants live ants on his burger but does not want to go hunting for ants himself, so he is waiting for the ants to come to the burger, at which point he will put the top bun back on and eat. I tell him that he will probably have better luck with that outside, and he says that's a good idea, thanks, and then goes outside with his hamburger, and that's the last I ever see of him.

CONFLUENCE OF [TEXTURE/テクスチャー] の集合　BY SAWAKO NAKAYASU AND MIWAKO OZAWA

Feeding strawberry shortcake to a [large/大きな], 実にとても大きな男に食べさせているのは man because, 当然その男が, himself of course unable of course, to eat on his own　自分で食べることが当然できないからだ.　The [first/最初]の重なり合い confluence は is taken at the 手で起きて hand, その手は which holds フォークを持っていて the fork, その上には upon which rests the [cake /ケーキ] が乗っていて, そのケーキはスポンジケーキとホイップクリームと人工着色した苺の一片で [できている/consisting of] sponge cake, whipped cream, and a small sliver of artificially reddened strawberry. とても小さなクッキーの抜き型が, ちょうど垂直方向にその瞬間を, 手, フォーク, ケーキと, 重なり合っているその一番上を流れるささやかな空気の間をも型抜いていく a very small cookie cutter goes right through into a vertical of this moment, through the hand, fork, and cake and even including the tender breath of air that is carried gently over the top of the moving confluence. Remove 型を外して, and 前菜用のお皿の上に乗せる place on the appetizer tray.

The hand with the fork with the [cake/ケーキ]を乗せたフォークを持った手は goes all the way into the interior of the　大きな, 実にとても大きな男の口の中に入って行き mouth of the large, very large indeed man himself, and in spite of the, この男が大きくて largeness of the man and the この手が小さいのにも smallness of this hand, にもかかわらず, the man finds it 男にとっては impossible to chew with a hand in his mouth 口の中で手を一緒に噛むのは無理で, でも, although one is hard-pressed to believe that a mere bite of strawberry shortcake could require much chewing 苺のショートケーキたった一口にそれほど咀嚼が必要なわけはない.

こんな感じでしばらく続ける

We continue in this fashion for a while.

Finally ついに男はペンを取って the man takes a pen and writes a note to [me/私]にメモを書き,

そこには優しい言葉で,この食べ方はあんまり素晴らしくもないんだけれど, と書いてある. 彼は時々, 苺を噛んだ時の触感と, 溶けたホイップクリームの触感の違いに気づいて, その先に何か快楽のヒントとなるものがあるはずだと察するのだけれど、まだそれを実感したことがない.

saying in gentle words that he is not having the most satisfying eating experience. Sometimes he notices the difference in texture between the give of the strawberry and the melted way of the whipped cream, and senses that there may be a hint of pleasure to be had somewhere in that direction, but he has yet to experience it for himself.

私の手は血が男の舌の先に垂れないようにとねじられ, 痺れている. My hand has been cramping from its contorted attempts to avoid getting blood on the top side of his tongue.

While we are both busy vowing that we will somehow try to continue, and improve upon, この食べること, 食べさせること, 食べさせられること the act of eating and feeding and getting fed, という行為をどうにか続けて向上させようと気が取られている間 に, we turn our heads and notice ふと振り返ると, 何かが視界から前菜用のお皿を取ってしまっていた that some third-party outside observer has removed the appetizer tray from sight,

私たちのおごりで楽しむ蟻の群れを見ないで済むようにね

so as to protect us from seeing the swarm of ants that are having a ball at our expense.

SCENES GATHERED FROM A CHINESE-ENGLISH DICTIONARY BY FRANCES CHUNG

clouds clearing away
simple clothing
rose-flower cake
coral chopsticks
night shining pearl
to gaze at the ocean and sigh
third day after a child's birth
moon clouded over
to give rice to the poor
husband of a wife's younger sister
to lie down undressed and sigh constantly
lunar mansion
to hold the knees and sing away
throw an embroidered ball in choosing a husband
to drown infants
first woman who taught Chinese people how to make
silk from silkworm
unknown hero born in the country
to enjoy chrysanthemums
fireflies at the window and snow on the table
with as many children as grasshoppers
anti-mosquito incense
incense sticks indicating time
double pillow used by newly married people
silence of three minutes
embroidered robes with axes drawn on them in black
and white

beautiful girl from a lower family
bamboo chair for mountain traveler
small open basket for holding rice
the yellow carp
white jasmine
kneel while incense burns
fried dough strips
a Buddhist word
bound feet of woman
to play at Chinese chess
a Taoist priest's robe
worms in books, clothes, or wood
carry dish with hands
songs of stilt workers
overfed baby vomits
coconut shell as ladle
to rub Chinese ink
whitish jade ear-plugs
a stroke to the right in writing
take off slipper
my dull mind is suddenly opened

背部

よるが色彩を食ひ

花たばはまがひものの飾を失ふ

日は輝く魚の如き葉に落ち

このひからびた嘲笑ふべき絶望の外に

育まれる無形の夢と樹を

卑賤な泥土のやうに跪き

切り倒された空間は

そのあしもとの雑草をくすぐる

煙草の脂で染まつた指が

うごめく闇を愛撫する

そして人が進み出る

NOTES

Unless otherwise specified, all poems, translations, and anti-translations are by **SAWAKO NAKAYASU** and-or **CHIKA SAGAWA**.

SAGAWA (左川—last name) **CHIKA** (ちか—first name) was born Kawasaki (川崎—last name) Ai (愛—first name) in 1911. The name "愛" can also be read "Chika," though she is also known to have been called "Ai." The characters for Sagawa (左川) mean "left river," a possible allusion to the Left Bank of Paris, while those in Kawasaki (川崎) mean "river promontory." The character "愛" means love, while the word "ちか" is an onomatopoeic word describing a flash of, or flashing, lights. Sagawa's first publications were translations, and at the time she published as Sagawa Chika (左川千賀), where "千賀"means "one thousand joys." From the point at which she published her translation of Harry Crosby's *Sleeping Together*, she modified her pen name to Sagawa Chika (左川ちか).

MASAKO HIRAIZUMI was born in 1962 in Tokyo, Japan. In 1985 she published her first book, *Differential Proprieties* (Shichosha). Each of her five published books demonstrates a markedly different style of writing, an example of which can be seen in her second book,

Night Fragments (Shoshi Yamada, 1991), which reflects her interest in avant-garde poetics of the Showa period. "Early Conversation" was published in *The Season of Poetry*, an anthology of poetry by participants in the International Poetry Festival in Lithuania (Open Letter, 2010).

HARRY CROSBY (1898—1929), the American poet and publisher of Black Sun Press, is not to be confused with the actor Harry Crosby, son of Bing Crosby. The poet Harry Crosby lived a wildly extravagant and decadent life as an expatriate in Paris in the 1920s, and with his press, published early works by James Joyce, D.H. Lawrence, Ezra Pound, Ernest Hemingway, and others. These English translations of Harry Crosby's poems are based on English-Japanese translations by Sagawa Chika, which were first published in *L'Esprit Nouveau* #3 in 1930, and recently collected in 『左川ちか翻訳詩』 (Sagawa Chika Collected Translations) published by Shinkaisha in 2011.

MINA LOY was an avant-garde poet and artist who was highly esteemed by many of her contemporaries, including Gertrude Stein, Ezra Pound, William Carlos Williams, and Marcel Duchamp. Her poem "Widow's Jazz" is loosely based on Sagawa's English-Japanese translation, first published in 『文学リーフレット』 (Literature Leaflet) in 1933 and later collected in 『左川ちか翻訳詩』 (Sagawa Chika Collected Translations) published by Shinkaisha in 2011.

STEVE WILLARD is a poet and musician in San Diego, California, and is the author of *Harm.* (University of California Press, 2007). "Flanky Pongo (Urla) #8" was published in the cartonera journal *TACOCAT UNO* (Greater Than Or Equal To Press, San Diego, CA— August 2011), published by Jeanine Webb.

FRANCES CHUNG was a Chinese-American New York School Poet. Her poems have been previously published in *Crazy Melon and Chinese Apple: The Poems of Frances Chung* (Wesleyan, 2000).

In the middle of writing this book, **MIWAKO OZAWA**, a friend and writer, left for the UK. The bilingual version of this poem (with Miwako Ozawa's Japanese translation) is a "reading copy" created for and read at the occasion of Miwako and Samson's farewell party, held at the Kamay Kitchen in Shimokitazawa, Tokyo on September 16, 2011. The poem and translation are forthcoming in the art journal *PINK*, published by Shinsuisha Records.

••••••

SO YOU SEE NOW IF YOU PUSH THROUGH THIS IDEA

That the existing teeming bee hives form an ideal brilliant order—emitted, rocked, and constructed among themselves. And then what clutches and happens is that it all gets modified, crushed, loosened by the whiskery introduction of the miracle new, the really new, young and nubile queen, distant and intimate, hopelessly among them.

But the existing hive was complete before the new queen arrived.

So then all this black-and-white means that in order for promise-less order to persist after the supervention of the new queen of sunshine, the carpeted quiet and whole existing ideal order must be just a tiny flower petal little bit altered. And so then the relations, proportions, and values of each sailor bee toward the whole are readjusted. This is rainbow conformity between the old and the new beard.

Whoever thinks this embroidered idea of unprotected order is okay will also gently admit that the carpet has bloomed profusely and that the past should be altered by the present as much as the present is directed by the past.

And woe is the silent silver bee who is unaware of these great difficulties and responsibilities.

•••••••

Are "プロムナアド (Puromunaado 2)" and "プロムナア
ド (Puromunaado 4)" in Chinese or are they not.

COVER ART: Photo of Sawako Nakayasu's tongue taken on Sunday, September 4, 2011 by Said Karlsson. The lizard, MJ, (named after Michael Jackson) currently resides with Kaori Kaneko and Hajime Kishii.

CHIKA SAGAWA was born in 1911 in Hokkaido, Japan. Arguably Japan's first female Modernist poet, Sagawa was a member of the lively community surrounding Kitasono Katue and was highly esteemed by her contemporaries. Stomach cancer took her life at the age of 25, at which point her poems were collected and edited by Ito Sei and published as 『左川ちか詩集』 (Sagawa Chika Poems) by Shourinsha in 1936. Later a more complete collected works, including her prose, in memoriam writings from poets, and a complete bibliography, was published as 『左川ちか全詩集』 (Collected Works of Sagawa Chika) by Shinkaisha in 1983. In 2010, her Collected Poems was republished by Shinkaisha, who also in 2011 published a new book collecting Sagawa's translations from English-language poetry, including poems by Charles Reznikoff and James Joyce.

SAWAKO NAKAYASU was born in Japan and has lived mostly in the US since the age of six. Her recent books are *Texture Notes* (Letter Machine Editions, 2010) and *Hurry Home Honey* (Burning Deck, 2009). Books of translations include *Time of Sky//Castles in the Air* by Ayane Kawata (Litmus Press, 2010) and *For the Fighting Spirit of the Walnut* by Takashi Hiraide (New Directions, 2008) which won the 2009 Best Translated Book Award from Three Percent, as well as *Four From Japan* (Litmus Press/ Belladonna Books, 2006) featuring female Japanese contemporary poets, and *To the Vast Blooming Sky* (Seeing Eye Books), a chapbook of poems by Chika Sagawa. Her translation of Sagawa's Collected Poems is forthcoming in 2013 from Canarium Books.

Cover photograph by Said Karlsson, 2011.
www.saidkarlsson.com

Design & typesetting by Drew Scott Swenhaugen & Sawako Nakayasu

ISBN-10: 0-9754468-5-1
ISBN-13: 978-0-9754468-5-0

Rogue Factorial is a rogue offshoot of Factorial Press.

Thanks to Drew Scott Swenhaugen, Jen Hofer, Joyelle McSweeney, Johannes Göransson, Jeffrey Angles, Hiromi Ito, Thalia Field, Steve Dolph, and Yelena Gluzman, whose direct and indirect influences combined over the course of about a week in September, leading to the production of this book.

Thanks, also, to Eiko, Masahiko, and Atsuhiko Nakayasu, Eugene Kang, and Marina Kang-Nakayasu. And to Tokyo University and Komaba Chiku Hoikuen.

Some of these works have been published in *Aufgabe*, *HOW2*, 『江古田文学』 (Ekota Bungaku), *Fascicle*, *Factorial*, *Calque*, *Poetry*, *Asymptote*, *Conduit*, *Encyclopedia*, *Vertebrae*, *Pink*, and *Texture Notes* (Letter Machine, 2010). Sagawa originals are from 『左川ちか全詩集』 (Sagawa Chika Collected Poems) published by Shinkaisha in 2010. Sagawa translations are from 『左川ちか翻訳詩集』 (Sagawa Chika Collected Translations) published by Shinkaisha in 2011.

Lightning Source UK Ltd.
Milton Keynes UK
UKHW011823090822
407073UK00004B/1124

9 780975 446850